Cream Cake

2022

Introduction

Birthday cake has an important meaning in human life

Birthday cake, also known as cream cake, cake is a dish with important and special meanings in birthday celebrations, weddings, weddings or important occasions of the year. However, birthday cakes today become more common in our lives, a birthday cake is a sweet dish in the form of a sponge cake that is covered with thick cream to increase the flavor and used to Make decorations for the cake more attractive and eye-catching. This is the most ornate, meticulous and delicate cake in the world.

Memorable Cake

Don't overlook the importance of a
good meal to start the day.

Simple puff pastry

1 time 1/2 tablespoon unsalted butter
1 time 1/2 tablespoon flour
1/2 cup whole milk
2 eggs (separate)
1/4 to 1/3 cup grated cheese
2 tablespoons Parmesan cheese
1/2 teaspoon ground mustard
1/4 teaspoon salt
1/4 teaspoon white pepper

Mixing multiple textures

Mix, experiment and have fun with the process.
The results may surprise you.

Delicious cakes are waiting for you!

Grape butter cake

INGREDIENTS:

- Flour No. 8 150 gr (or number 11 all-purpose flour)
- Unsalted Butter 150 gr
- Baking powder 2 teaspoons (baking powder)
- Raisins 25 gr, Chicken eggs 3
- Sliced almonds 10 gr (To decorate)
- Fresh milk without sugar 40 ml
- Vanilla essence 1 teaspoon, Rum 25 ml
- Salt 1/2 teaspoon, Sugar 130 gr

INSTRUCTIONS:

- Step 1: Prepare the ingredients
- First, soak 25g of raisins with 25ml of rum for 15 minutes. After 15 minutes, take out the grapes to drain.
- Next, put in a bowl: 150g flour, 2 teaspoons baking powder, 1/2 teaspoon salt and mix well. Then, you filter this flour mixture through a sieve until smooth.

- Step 2: Beat the butter and egg mixture
- Place 150g unsalted butter in a new bowl and beat butter on medium speed for about 20 seconds. Then, slowly add 130g of sugar to the bowl of butter, beat and beat until the mixture is smooth, and the butter turns white.
- Next, add 3 eggs in turn to the bowl and continue beating until the mixture is smooth.
- Outward remittance: Butter needs to be softened at room temperature, pressed with your hands to be soft enough but not to the point of mushy or watery.
- It is important to beat the butter thoroughly because the cake swells and porosity is due to the air bubbles in the butter when whipping.

- Step 3: Make the sponge cake mix
- Add to the bowl of butter: dry powder mixture in Step 1, 40ml of unsweetened fresh milk, 1 teaspoon of vanilla essence.

- Mix well with a mixer on low speed until fully combined.
- Finally, put the soaked raisins in the flour bowl, mix again and you're done.
- Small tip: To prevent the cake from hardening, you should not mix the dough for too long!

- Step 4: Bake
- Preheat the oven at 155 degrees Celsius for 10 minutes with 2 fire on top and bottom, with convection fan.
- Prepare a baking pan lined with parchment paper, then spread the dough evenly and sprinkle some sliced almonds on top.
- Next, put the cake in the oven and bake it at 155 degrees Celsius for 40 - 55 minutes (depending on the oven capacity).

- Step 5: Finish product
- The grape butter cake has an extremely attractive aroma, the cake when eaten is soft, sweet and fatty, mixed with the sour taste of raisins and the flesh of almonds, delicious, delicious.

Soufflé vani

INGREDIENTS:

- Chicken eggs 4 eggs(Yellow)
- Sugar 30 gr
- Flour No. 8 25 gr
- Unsalted Butter 35 gr
- Fresh milk without sugar 165 gr
- Vanilla 1/4 teaspoon
- Meringue 60 gr
- (Egg white 4 pcs + Sugar 40g)

INSTRUCTIONS:

- Step 1: Brush butter and sugar into the baking pan
- First, use a brush to spread a layer of butter into the baking pan. Then, put sugar in, coat a thin layer so that the sugar adheres evenly to the mold.

- Step 2: Mix cake dough
- Put 4 egg yolks, 30g sugar in a bowl, then use a spatula to stir the mixture well.
- Sift 25g of baking powder into the egg mixture. Then continue to mix until the mixture is smooth.

- Step 3: Melt butter
- You put in the pot 35g unsalted butter with 165g fresh milk without sugar and 1/4 teaspoon vanilla.
- Next, put the pot on the stove and cook over low heat and stir until the mixture is combined.

- Step 4: Stir the mixture on the stove
- Slowly add the melted butter to the batter and stir with a spatula.
- Continue to cook the above mixture over low heat and continue to stir with a spatula until the mixture is smooth, slightly thick.

- Step 5: Mix the mixture with Meringue
- First, take 4 egg whites and separate them in a bowl, beat with a mixer at low speed until the eggs are foamy like soap.
- Divide 40g of sugar into 3 parts, slowly add each part and beat until dissolved. Beat each sugar for about 30 seconds on low speed, then add the next sugar to beat.
- When adding the last sugar to the eggs, turn on the mixer at high speed, beat the eggs until the eggs are stiff, flexible, glossy and creamy, lift the whisk to create a vertical peak.
- You divide the Meringue into 4 parts, add the first 2 parts to the mixture and then gently stir with a spatula until all ingredients are combined.
- Next, you add the above mixture to the remaining 2 Meringue parts and then use a flat spatula to gently mix the mixture from bottom to top. Bring the spatula to the bottom of the bowl, lift the heavy ingredients, and fold aside. Continue until the mixture becomes smooth.
- Note: do not stick the yolk because the yolk contains a lot of fat, which limits the formation and the air bubbles from the white easily escape. Thus, you will not be able to make delicious and successful cakes.

- Step 6: Bake
- Pour the flour mixture slowly into the cake pan.
- Preheat oven to 190 degrees Celsius for 10 minutes. Then, put the cake in the oven at 190 degrees Celsius for 10 minutes. Next, reduce the oven temperature to 180 degrees C and continue to bake for 5 minutes is satisfactory.

- Step 7: Finished product
- Souffle cake has a soft, melted base with a sweet, buttery taste. You can serve the cake with strawberry jam, raspberry or fresh cream to make the cake more delicious.

Chocolate Mousse

- Ingredients for Chocolate Mousse

- Whipping cream 100 gr
- Pure cocoa powder 20 gr
- Fresh milk 550 gr (unsweetened or sweetened)
- Sugar 60 gr
- Dark chocolate chips 100 gr

- How to make Chocolate Mousse without gelatin

- 1 Stir together cocoa powder and Whipping Cream
- First, put 100g of Whipping Cream in a bowl, heat it in a water bath for warm whipping, do not boil. (about 40 50 degrees).
- Next, add in the warmed Whipping 20g pure cocoa powder and then use a spatula to mix well.

- 2 Mix cocoa with milk
- Put 550g (ml) of fresh milk, 60g of sugar and 20g of cornstarch in a large bowl. Then add the mixed cocoa Whipping mixture into the bowl. Then use a spatula to stir the mixture evenly and evenly.

- 3 Heat the mixture
- After stirring the mixture, you filter the mixture and then put it in a pot, put on the stove to boil over low heat.
- While boiling the mixture, use a spatula to constantly stir the mixture evenly, this helps to avoid burning the milk at the bottom of the pot.
- Boil for about 5 minutes, add 100g of dark chocolate chips to the pot and continue stirring until the chocolate is completely melted.
- When the mixture thickens and thickens, stirring is heavy, then turn off the stove.
- Note: Do not heat the milk on high heat because it will burn the milk at the bottom of the pot and make the mixture uneven. It will be quite tiring, but you need to stir the mixture constantly to avoid clumping.

- 4 Fine filtration and molding
- Prepare a deep mold, cut the mold with parchment paper and line it up. Lining parchment paper in the mold will make it easier to remove the cake.
- Pour the mixture slowly through the sieve, filtering the mixture will help you get a mousse cake that is both smooth and avoids leaving air bubbles that cause pitting.
- Next, let the cake cool in the refrigerator for 6 hours to completely freeze.
- Note: Because the mixture is quite thick, you should work hard to pour it slowly, avoid pouring it quickly, it will easily spill the mousse out.

- 5 Remove the cake from the mold
- After freezing the cake in the refrigerator, you bring the cake outside. Use a plate larger than the cake pan and place it face down on the pan. Then gently turn the cake pan upside down to remove the cake.
- The mousse is quite soft, so gently remove the parchment paper.
- Next, use a little cocoa powder sprinkled lightly on the cake to decorate. So you have finished the Chocolate Mousse cake.

- 6 Finished Products
- No need to use Gelatin coagulant powder, you can still make a delicious, smooth, and delicious Mousse cake for your family. It's too simple, isn't it, what are you waiting for, roll up your sleeves and go to the kitchen to make a cake for the family.

Orange cake

- Ingredients

- American yellow oranges 5 (American Navel orange)
- Whipping cream 440 g
- Sugar 44 g
- Orange food coloring 2 g
- Sugar water 20 ml
- Cake mold 15 cm 1 piece

- Implementation tools
- Egg beater

- How to make Orange Cake

- 1 Preliminary processing of oranges
- When you buy oranges, soak them in diluted mosquito water for about 10 minutes and then wash them with clean water.
- You use the tip of the knife to cut a small circle around the stem and then remove the circle.
- Then you put the knife into 6 around the orange (note that you only cut about 2-3 mm deep in the orange peel). Then you use your hands to separate each piece of the peel from the orange.
- When you have finished peeling the oranges, use a knife to cut the oranges in half and then cut 1 piece into 0.5 cm thin slices. The remaining 5 fruits you cut the edge of the segment, leave a little at the tip of the nose to make the orange piece beautiful.

- 2 Whipping cream
- You put 400g of whipping cream in a bowl, add 40g of sugar, use an electric mixer to beat at low to high speed until the cream is soft and has a clear creamy texture, lift the spatula down.
- In another bowl, whip 40 g whipping cream, 4 g sugar, 2 drops orange food coloring.

- 3 Matching cake
- Cake mold 15 6 cm thick, you cut circles into 3 (each about 2 cm thick). Or you can decorate according to the size of the cake you have available.
- You put the first piece of cake on the turntable, put a thin layer of sugar water on the cake, take about 2 tablespoons of whipped cream, use a knife to rub it, rub it with and arrange the oranges.
- Continue to add 2 tablespoons of whipped cream and then add the sponge cake, do the same to the third cake layer.
- Then you take the whipped cream to cover the cake and the surface of the cake, use a knife to rub it with cream.

- 4 Cake decorations
- You take the orange whipped cream around the cake, then use a smooth knife to rub it around the cake.
- Then cleverly catch a circle of cream around the surface of the cake, then arrange the orange part inside the circle, decorate with a few mint leaves and you're done.
- How to store cakes:

- Let the cake cool completely, then use a sealed plastic bag or a lidded box to preserve the cake.
- Store at room temperature if it's cool (below 20 degrees Celsius) or refrigerate and use within 3 days.

Strawberry cake

- Ingredients for making strawberry cake

- All-purpose flour 110 gr
- Corn starch 30 gr
- Strawberries 220 gr
- 7 chicken eggs (whole shell is 342g)
- Unsalted unsalted butter 70 gr
- Whipping cream 300 ml

- Sugar 220 gr
- Salt 1 gr
- Vanilla essence 3 ml
- Lemon juice 1 little

- Implementation tools
- Oven, whisk, whisk, bowl, pot, sieve,...

- How to make Strawberry cream cake (gato cake)

- 1 Strawberry processing
- Strawberries soak in dilute salt water for a few minutes, then wash, drain and cut in half, remove the stem.

- 2 Cooking strawberry jam
- After preparing strawberries, you leave about 4 fruits for decoration, the rest, you mix with 100g of sugar for about 30 minutes and then bring it to cook.
- Cook the strawberries over medium heat until the strawberries are soft. Then you filter it through a sieve, use a spoon to mash the strawberries and filter out the residue.
- Cover the jam and keep it in the fridge.

- 3 Beat egg whites
- Separate egg whites and egg yolks. Divide 120g of sugar into 3 equal parts.
- Using an electric mixer, beat egg whites into large soapy bubbles, then add a few drops of lemon juice, 1g of salt and 1/3 of the sugar and beat on low speed.

- After 30 seconds, put the sugar in once until it's all gone, then increase the engine speed to high. Beat until the whites are fluffy and have stiff peaks.

- 4 Mix the cake batter
- In a bowl, add 70ml of unsweetened fresh milk and 70gr of melted butter, 3ml of vanilla essence, and mix well with a spatula. Next, sift in 110g of flour and 30g of corn starch and mix until the mixture is homogeneous.
- Divide the beaten egg whites into 3 equal parts.
- Add 1/3 of the beaten egg whites to the yolk mixture. Quickly fold the mix (scratch and flip from the bottom) to blend the ingredients, do the same with the remaining 2 egg whites to get a homogeneous mixture.

- Tip: When mixing the ingredients with the whipped whites, mix them gently to avoid breaking the air bubbles that prevent the cake from blooming.

- 5 Molding and baking
- Move the bracket down to the last 4th groove of the oven (if you are using a 48 liter 4-slot oven). Preheat the oven to 175 degrees Celsius for 15 minutes before baking to allow the oven to stabilize. Lined with parchment paper (removable molds do not need to be lined with stencils).

- Pour the cake batter into the pan, gently knock the mold down on a flat surface and place in the oven. Lower the heat to 150 degrees C and bake for 80 minutes 2 fire on the bottom with a convection fan.
- When the cake is done baking, open the oven door a little, wait 10 minutes, then take it out. Wait for the cake to cool, then remove from the mold and divide the cake into 3 layers.

- 6 Whip the whipping cream and spread it on the cake
- Put the whisk in the freezer for about 30 minutes, then bring out and beat 300ml of whipping cream. Beat until smooth, then stop.
- Small tip: If you don't have liquid whipping cream, you can use 150g of whipping cream powder mixed with 350ml of unsweetened fresh milk and whisk it instead.
- Lay down the first layer of cake, cover with a layer of cooked strawberry jam, then place the second layer of cake on top.
- Continue to spread whipping cream and arrange fresh strawberries, cut 1/2 of them, then spread whipping cream and smooth.
- Put the 3rd cake layer on top, then spread whipping cream on top and smooth the surface of the cake.
- Garnish with a layer of strawberries on top, then put in the refrigerator and use gradually.
- Outward remittance:
- Place the whisk in the fridge to chill, making it easy to whip the whipping cream.

- You can decorate it to your liking.
- Before each layer of cake is covered with cream or strawberries, a thin layer of sugar syrup or unsweetened fresh milk must be spread to keep the cake sugar soft, moist and not dry.

- 7 Finished Products
- Strawberry cream cake is delicious and very beautiful to look at. The cake is soft and sweet mixed with sweet and sour strawberry jam. Ripe strawberries, sour and sour, eaten with cream cakes both enhance the flavor of the cake and help make the cake less boring.

- Tips for successful implementation
- No matter what cake you bake, you must preheat the oven first to stabilize the heat and the cake will be more beautiful. The oven heating temperature is 15 - 30°C higher than the baking temperature.
- After the cake is molded, it must be baked immediately without leaving it for a long time, otherwise the cake will easily concave the bottom and tighten the waist.
- High-heat baking will spoil the cake even if the egg whites are beaten well.
- The dough should not be too loose, the whites must be beaten well otherwise the cake will have a hard egg layer on the bottom.
- After baking, the cake will have a little egg smell, let it cool and then put it in the refrigerator to make it more delicious.

Coconut cream cake

- Ingredients
-
- All-purpose flour 60 gr
- Gelatin powder 8 gr
- Cinnamon powder 1/2 teaspoon
- Ginger powder 1/2 teaspoon
- Nutmeg powder 1/4 teaspoon
- Clove powder 1/8 teaspoon
- Baking powder 1/2 teaspoon
- Baking soda 1/4 teaspoon

- Ginger biscuits 70 gr
- Coconut grated 35 gr
- Coconut ice cream 200 gr
- Whipping cream 405 ml
- Molasses 30 ml
- Coconut milk 200 ml
- White chocolate 120 gr

- Sugar 130 gr
- Black sugar 30 gr
- 1 little rosemary leaves
- Coconut truffles 1 piece
- Small round candy 16 gr

- Rum 1 teaspoon
- 1 chicken egg
- Cooking oil 42 ml
- Salt 1/2 teaspoon

- How to make Coconut Cream Cake

- 1 Mix baking powder
- First, you sift in a bowl: 60g flour, 1/2 teaspoon cinnamon powder, 1/4 teaspoon salt, 1/2 teaspoon ginger powder, 1/4 teaspoon nutmeg powder, 1/4 teaspoon baking soda, 1/2 teaspoon baking powder, 1/8 teaspoon clove powder. Then, use a spatula to mix well.

- 2 Beat egg mixture
- Next, take another bowl and put in 1 egg, 30g sugar, 30g black sugar. Use the mixer on medium speed until the mixture is smooth and creamy.
- Next, slowly add 42ml of oil to the egg bowl, 1 teaspoon of rum and continue to mix with a mixer.
- Finally, add 30ml of molasses, mix well one more time and you're done.

- 3 Mix the cake mix
- Slowly add the dry flour mixture to the egg bowl, mixing while mixing on low speed until the mixture is smooth and well combined.

- 4 Molding and baking
- Preheat oven to 180 degrees Celsius for 15 minutes. Prepare a cake pan lined with parchment paper, pour in the dough and bake for 10-12 minutes at 180 degrees Celsius.

- 5 Make the coconut gingerbread filling
- Put in a pot 30g sugar, 15ml water and boil over low heat until the sugar boils and starts to turn light brown.
- At this point, you immediately add 35 grams of grated coconut and mix well on low heat for another 1 minute. Next, add in the mixture of grated coconut 70g of grated gingerbread, 16g of small round candies and mix well.
- Next, put in a new bowl 120g chopped white chocolate, 45ml whipping cream. Then, heat the chocolate in a pot of boiling water until the chocolate melts.
- Next, pour the chocolate into the grated coconut mixture and mix once more.

- 6 Molding and cooling
- Remove the sponge cake from the mold, then spread the coconut ginger mixture evenly on the face, remember to leave the outer edge about 6mm.

- Next, wrap the outside of the cake in a separate mold, lined the inside of the mold with a layer of flexible plastic and then chill in the refrigerator.

- 7 Make the coconut mousse
- Put 8g gelatin powder in a bowl, 45ml cold water, stir well, then soak for 10 minutes for gelatin to swell.
- Put the pot on the stove, add 200ml of coconut milk, 70g of sugar, 1/4 teaspoon of salt, 200g of coconut cream. Stir the mixture over medium heat until warm, sugar and cream completely dissolved.
- Next, pour the coconut milk mixture into a bowl, add the soaked gelatin and stir until the gelatin dissolves.
- In another bowl, add 360ml of whipping cream and beat with a mixer until the cream is soft, creating a vertical peak but curved downwards.
- Next, pour the coconut milk mixture into the bowl of whipping cream, mix again by machine one more time and it's done.

- 8 Casting and cooling
- Pour all the coconut cream mixture into the prepared cake mold, then freeze in the refrigerator for 4-6 hours or overnight.

- 9 Decorate the gingerbread coconut cake
- Finally, remove the mold from the cake, garnish with some coconut truffles, ginger biscuits, rosemary leaves, sprinkle with more grated coconut and you're done.

- 10 Finished Products
- Coconut cream cake has a simple decoration but is extremely delicate and beautiful. Inside is a soft, fragrant cake that blends with a layer of attractive sweet cream. In addition, you will also feel the crunchiness, the characteristic aroma from the layer of coconut gingerbread, delicious, delicious.

Durian cream cake

- Ingredients for making Durian Cream Cake

- Durian 500 gr
- Sugar 25 gr
- Fresh milk without sugar 170 ml
- Whipping cream 500 ml
- 1 sponge cake (divided into 3 equal parts)
- Alum sugar 1 little
- 1 leaf mint

- How to make Durian Cream Cake

- 1 Cook durian with milk
- First, you put 500gr of durian, 25gr of sugar and 170ml of unsweetened fresh milk into the pot, turn on the heat, then put the pot on the stove.
- Use a spatula to stir for about 5 minutes and cook until well combined. When the mixture boils, shake the pot gently for about 2 minutes, then put the milk durian mixture in a bowl to cool.

- 2 Puree the durian mixture
- Next, use a hand blender to puree the durian mixture in a bowl for about 3 minutes until the mixture becomes smooth and fine.

- 3 Make durian cake ice cream
- Put 500ml of whipping cream in a bowl, use an electric mixer to beat the cream on slow speed for 1 minute and beat at high speed for 9 minutes until the whipping cream becomes stiff and smooth.
- Next, you put all 500ml of whipped cream into the bowl of the pureed durian mixture, use a flat spatula to mix all the ingredients together and then put them in the ice cream bag.

- 4 Make durian cream cake
- Prepare a turntable and place a tray on the tabletop. Put in the tray a round sponge cake, about 2 fingers thick.

- One hand holds the prepared ice cream bag so that the handle is perpendicular to the cake surface, the mouth of the ice cream bag is in the center of the cake surface. One hand grabs the turntable and turns it slightly. The hand holding the ice cream bag uses force to gently squeeze the cream to flow out in circles from the inside to the outside to the end of the cake.
- Next, hold a knife parallel to the surface of the cake with one hand, the tip of the knife is placed in the middle of the cake, the knife surface lightly touches the cream layer, with one hand gently rotates the turntable, gently presses the knife to spread the durian cream evenly. all over the cake, forming a flat icing.
- Continue, you put the 2nd sponge cake on and do the same as the first layer. To the 3rd layer of sponge cake, you put all the remaining durian cream on the cake and then use a knife to spread the layer of cream over the cake.

- 5 Finished Products
- Finally, you sprinkle the top of the cream with a little rock sugar and stick a small mint leaf in the center of the cake for decoration. So we have finished the durian cream cake.
- The remaining durian cream flows down the cake to create a beautiful cream wave. The green color of the mint leaves in the middle, dotted on the white cream make the cake look outstanding.
- Soft sponge cake, greasy, sweet durian cream, eat a piece, you will feel the durian flavor spreading in your mouth. It's really delicious!

Chocolate strawberry cake

- Ingredients

- Cake flour 53 gr
- Cornstarch 10 gr
- Cocoa powder 7 gr
- Unsalted Butter 17 gr
- Fresh milk 280 ml
- Sugar 115 gr
- Vanilla essence 4 ml
- Strawberry puree 30 gr
- Whipping cream 80 gr (whisked)
- 1 handful fresh strawberries (for garnish)
- Ganache (to cover the cake) 1
- (includes 70g chocolate and 35g whipping cream)

- Gelatin 1 leaf (2g)
- Eggs 95 gr
- Egg yolk 3 pieces
- Corn syrup 7 ml

- How to make Heart-shaped Chocolate Strawberry Cake

- 1 Beat eggs
- Put in a bowl 95gr eggs, 65g sugar, 7ml corn syrup, then place this bowl in a pot of hot water about 80 degrees Celsius.
- Use a spatula to stir until the mixture is combined, reaching 40 degrees Celsius, then remove the bowl from the pot of water.
- Add 2ml vanilla essence to the bowl, beat with an electric mixer on medium speed for about 3 minutes.
- Next, turn to the lowest speed, beat for 2 minutes until the mixture is fluffy, turns ivory white, lift the fluff like a ribbon (Ribbon Stage State).
- Pro tip: Warming the eggs will help the eggs to fluff faster, and the eggs will be more structurally stable. However, you should only warm the eggs to about 40 - 50 degrees Celsius, otherwise the eggs will be overcooked and less fluffy.

- 2 Mix cake batter
- Sift 100g flour, 7g cocoa powder into the beaten egg mixture.

- Use a spatula to gently mix the mixture from bottom to top. Bring the spatula to the bottom of the bowl, push the ingredients up, and fold to the side. Continue until the mixture is combined.
- Melt 17g unsalted butter and 30ml fresh milk, then take a little cake flour mixture into the butter mixture and stir well.
- Next, pour the butter mixture back into the cake batter and continue to fold it until blended.
-
- 3 Molding and baking
- Preheat oven to 180 degrees Celsius for 15 minutes.
- Prepare a cake pan lined with parchment paper, then pour the dough and bake for 25 minutes at 180 degrees Celsius.
-
- 4 Make custard custard cream
- In a bowl, add 3 egg yolks, 50g sugar, 10g cornstarch and stir well to combine.
- Heat the mixture of 250ml milk, 2ml vanilla essence, then slowly pour into the egg mixture and continue to stir to combine.
- Put the pot on the stove, pour in the egg and milk mixture and stir on low until thickened.
- Pour the mixture into a bowl, cover with cling film and let cool.

- 5 Mix strawberry ice cream
- Softly soak 1 gelatin leaf in a cup of ice water for 10 minutes, then squeeze out the water and spin for 10 seconds in the microwave to melt.
- Put in a bowl 80g custard cream, 30g strawberry puree, melted gelatin and stir well.
- Next, you add 80g of whipping cream, which has been lightly whipped and then gently mix to combine.
- Tip: Whipping cream will be lightly whipped and will have a slightly thickened state, may create a texture but not clear and when lifting the beater, it will not create a peak.

- 6 Cut the cake core and decorate with strawberries
- Cut the sponge cake into several round pieces about 1 inch thick. Then, you use a heart-shaped mold to shape the cake.
- Shape and fix the mica into a heart shape and place it inside the cake mold. Note, the height of the mica will be about 1 inch higher than the mouth of the mold.
- First, you put 1 piece of cake inside, then arrange the sliced strawberries around the mold.
- Next, you inject the strawberry cream and then sprinkle some fresh chopped strawberries on your face. Then, cover the entire cake with another layer of strawberry cream.

- Finally, put 1 piece of sponge cake on top, sprinkle the chocolate cream (Ganache) evenly on top and you're done. Place the cake in the fridge for 2-3 hours to set.
- Pro tip: Ganache is made by mixing 70g of melted chocolate with 35g of whipping cream.

- 7 Finished Products
- Strawberry cream cake has a lovely shape, the cake is soft and smooth, the sponge is blended with the layer of sweet and fatty strawberry cream, fresh strawberries are succulent, slightly sour, extremely delicious.

Corn cake

- Ingredients for Corn Cream Cake

- American corn 2 pieces
- Cream cheese 30 gr
- Whipping cream 400 gr
- Flour No. 8 65 gr
- Unsalted butter 20 gr
- Fresh milk 100 ml
- Sugar 95 gr
- Salt 2 gr

- Chicken eggs 5 eggs
- Cooking oil 50 ml
- 1 piece white chocolate
- 1 handful almonds (sliced)

- How to make Corn Cake
-
- 1 Preliminary processing of corn
- Peel off the skin and beard of the corn and wash it well.
- Put the pot on the stove, add 1 liter of water, then bring the pre-prepared corn to boil.
- After the corn cools, use a knife to cut the kernels off.

- 2 Grind corn milk
- Put in a blender 50ml of corn boiled water, 100ml of fresh milk, 250g of corn kernels and then puree the mixture.
- Next, strain the mixture through a sieve to remove the lint.
- Note: Remember to leave 50g of corn kernels to decorate the cake!

- 3 Cook corn cream sauce
- Put the pot on the stove, add the ground corn, 20g unsalted butter, 30g cream cheese.
- Stir the mixture over low heat until the butter and cheese melt.
- Mix 100g of whipping cream with 5g of flour, then put this mixture into the pot of cream of corn and stir well.
- Next, add 15g of sugar, 2g of salt, stir again and you're done.

- 4 Make a sponge cake
- Put in a bowl 5 egg yolks, 50ml of cooking oil and stir the mixture. Next, sift 60g of flour into the bowl and mix well to combine.
- Then, you add 50g of corn cream sauce cooked in step 3 into the bowl of egg powder and continue to mix well.
- Small tip: Remember to keep the remaining corn cream sauce to decorate the cake!
- In a new bowl, add 5 egg whites, and beat on low speed with an electric mixer until foamy bubbles form.
- Divide 50g of sugar into 3 parts, add each part and beat until dissolved. Beat each sugar for about 30 seconds on low speed, then add the next sugar to beat.
- When adding the last sugar to the eggs, turn on the mixer at high speed, beat the eggs until the eggs are soft, creamy, the mixture is flexible, glossy and smooth, lift the whisk to create a vertical top but turn it down.
- Note: Divide the sugar into 2 or 3 parts and add it little by little. Avoid putting in all at once.
- The whites when beaten must be at room temperature (if taken from the refrigerator) and the whites must be free from other dirt or fats.
- Divide the beaten egg whites into three parts. First, you add part of the egg white to the egg yolk mixture, then gently stir all the ingredients with a whisk.

- Put the mixture just stirred into the bowl of egg whites and then use a spatula to gently mix the mixture from bottom to top. Bring the spatula to the bottom of the bowl, push the ingredients up, and fold to the side. Continue until the mixture becomes smooth.
- Preheat oven to 160 degrees Celsius for 15 minutes. Then, pour the flour mixture into a mold lined with parchment paper and bake at 150 - 160 degrees C for 50 - 60 minutes.

- 5 Make ice cream
- In a bowl, add 30 grams of sugar, 300 grams of whipping cream, and beat with a mixer until soft and fluffy, creating a vertical peak but turning down.
- Then, you divide the corn cream sauce mixture into 2 parts, put 1 part in a bowl of fresh cream and mix well with a flat spatula.

- 6 Shaping
- Cut the cake core into 2-3 round pieces. First, you cover the first piece of cake with a layer of corn cream sauce, sprinkle some more boiled corn, then continue to cover it with another layer of corn cream.
- Next, place the second cake on top and repeat the coating until the last piece.
- When you come to the last piece of cake, you cover the cake with corn cream and sprinkle with a little white chocolate, sliced almonds and boiled corn and you're done.

- 7 Finished Products
- Corn cream cake has a greasy coating, fragrant with corn flavor, the inner cake is soft and spongy mixed with sweet and fatty cream sauce, extremely attractive and delicious.

Strawberry tart

INGREDIENTS:

- All-purpose flour 100 gr
- Cornstarch 25 gr
- Strawberry jam 110 gr
- Whipping cream 100 ml
- Coconut milk 50 ml
- Fresh milk without sugar 100 ml
- Unsalted Butter 77 gr
- Chicken eggs 3
- Salt 1/2 teaspoon
- Sugar 45 gr

INSTRUCTIONS:

- Step1: Knead and knead the dough
- First of all, you need to separate 1 egg and put it in a separate bowl (rice bowl). Next, use a whisk and beat the yolks and egg whites together and only take 25g of eggs to make the cake.
- Next, prepare a large bowl and add 100g of flour, 1/2 teaspoon of salt, 15g of sugar, 70g of unsalted butter, then knead well with your hands so that the butter is evenly absorbed into the dough for about 3-4 minutes.
- After the ingredients have been mixed together, slowly add 25g of eggs while kneading the dough evenly. You continue to knead for about 7-10 minutes so that the mixture becomes a smooth dough and no longer sticks to your hands.
- Finally, cover the dough with cling film and put it in the refrigerator to rest for about 45 minutes.
- Tip: Before making the cake, remember to chill the butter in the refrigerator first!

- Step 2: Shape and bake the cake base for the 1st time
- After 45 minutes, take out the dough and knead it again for about 2-3 minutes. Next, you roll the dough very thin and cut the dough into round slices so that the diameter of the dough is larger than the diameter of the cake mold.
- You put each slice of dough into the mold and use your hands to gently press the cake base to fit the mold and about 0.3 cm high.

- Next, you put the dough tray in the freezer for 2 hours. Then, you take out the dough, line the pre-cut parchment paper on each surface of the cake bases and put a little rice on top to fix.
- You preheat the oven for 10 minutes to 170 degrees Celsius first. Next, you bake the cake base for about 10 minutes with the same temperature and 2 fire mode.
- Pro tip: After shaping, you should use a fork and poke small holes in the surface of the dough so that when baking, the cake base can escape air, avoiding blistering.
- Step 3: Bake the cake base for the 2nd time
- After 10 minutes, remove the cake from the oven and remove the parchment paper and rice. In the next step, you continue to bake the cake base for the second time with a temperature of 170 degrees Celsius and the 2-fire mode like the first time about 5 minutes and it's done!

- Step 4: Make egg cream mixture
- To make the cream filling, separate 2 egg yolks and place them in a large bowl. You add 30g of sugar to the mix, use a whisk and beat well for about 3 minutes until the sugar dissolves.
- Next, you put 25g of cornstarch into the egg mixture through a sieve to make the flour smoother.
- You continue to use a whisk and stir the mixture by hand for about 7 minutes to combine the ingredients.

- Step 5: Melt the strawberry jam mixture
- You prepare a small pot and put in 100ml of fresh milk, 50ml of coconut milk and 100ml of whipping cream, then boil the mixture for about 3-4 minutes with medium heat until warm.
- Then, slowly add the boiled milk to the egg cream prepared in the above step and stir well.
- Next, you put the mixture into the pot and cook over medium heat for about 7 minutes until it thickens. While cooking, remember to stir constantly to avoid burning!
- After the mixture thickens, turn off the heat and add 7g unsalted butter and stir well for about 3 minutes.
- Next, you add 100g of strawberry jam to the mix and stir well, the cream filling is done!
- Put the strawberry jam in a bowl and cover with cling film and let it cool for about 10 minutes.

- Step 6: Complete
- In this last step, you cleverly put each spoon of strawberry jam arbitrarily into the cake base and top it with a little strawberry jam and the strawberry tart is complete!

MONT BLANC CAKE

MATERIALS:

- Wheat flour: 400g
- Almond powder: 200g
- Sugar: 420g
- Chicken eggs: 8 eggs
- Melted butter: 80g
- Cold Butter: 350g
- Cream cheese: 300g
- Whipping cream: 1kg
- Salt: 6g
- Water: 20ml

INSTRUCTIONS FOR MAKING MONT BLANC:

- MAKING THE TART
- Put 6g of salt, 20ml of water and 20g of sugar in a small bowl and stir until dissolved. Add this mixture to the prepared flour, add 2 eggs and beat with a whisk until the mixture is uniform.
- Use your hands to mix the dough
- Use your hands to mix the cake flour and butter into a smooth dough
- Next, add 200g of cold butter, mix the dough with your hands and knead it into a smooth dough. Use dry flour to cover the surface with a layer of flour to prevent sticking, knead the dough to make it evenly, then cover the dough with plastic wrap and let it rest in the refrigerator for 30 minutes.

- CAKE FOR THE CAKE
- After the dough is finished, spread the dry flour to make the dough, then cut the dough into small pieces. Use your hands to roll the dough into a small circle. Then pour the dough into the tart pan. Use two thumbs to gently press the dough down in the shape of a nice mold.

- MAKING THE CAKE
- In a bowl of 180g sugar, add 6 eggs, beat well until the sugar has dissolved and the mixture is homogeneous.

- Add 200ml of whipping cream to the mixture, continue to stir the mixture until homogeneous. Then pass the mixture through a sieve until smooth. Add the melted butter, 50g of almond flour and continue stirring until the mixture is uniform and smooth.

- SUPPLY INTO THE TART
- Pour the cake mixture just made into the tart base, but do not overfill but leave a space for the cake to expand.

- THE SECRETS OF BREAKING DELICIOUS CAKES
- Put the cake mold on a baking tray, turn on the oven at 200 degrees Celsius to preheat about 10-15 minutes. Then put the cake in the oven for 15 minutes until the cake is nicely golden.

- MAKING CHEESE CREAM
- Beat 60g sugar with 600g whipping cream until soft peaks form.
- Beat 300g cream cheese on a bowl of ice cold water, then mix the cream cheese into the whipping cream mixture and beat until smooth again. Place the mixture in the fridge for about 30 minutes.

- MAKING ALMOND CREAM
- Whip 200g whipping cream, add 160g sugar and 150g butter until homogeneous, add 5ml of barcadi, 10ml of amabetto, continue to beat.

- Add the whipped whipping cream, and beat one more time until the mixture is smooth. Add 150g of almond flour, use a spatula to mix the cream together.

- FINISHING THE CAKE
- Put the cream cheese filling and almond cream filling into the ice cream bag, then use the cream tip to shape with the cream cheese filling on the top of the cake. The almond cream part cuts the top of the ice cream bag to create a small thread, then evenly applies the cream cheese filling to create a beautiful shape. Decorate the cake and enjoy.

Durian cheese cake

INGREDIENTS:

- 1 bag of Sampa (aka Lady Fingers)
- 480g cream cheese
- 250g heavy cream fresh cream
- 135g sugar
- 3 ripe mangoes
- 100ml mango juice
- The jelly topping on the cake:
- 220ml mango juice
- 30g of gelatin
- 120ml boiling water
- 15ml of rum (optional)

INSTRUCTIONS:

- Step 1: Prepare a removable base mold - aka Spring-form. Dip each Sampa cake into the mango juice, then arrange the cakes along the sides of the mold and seal the bottom of the mold. Peel mango, cut into small squares, refrigerate.

- Step 2: Place cream cheese and sugar in a bowl, beat well. Cool fresh cream, use a stiff beater.
- Step 2a: Mix the fresh cream into the cream cheese you whipped until you get a smooth paste.
- Step 2b: Pour in the mango cut into small squares, mix well.

- Step 3: Pour all the cream into the mold that already has Sampa cake, spread it evenly and store it in the refrigerator.

- Step 4: Put the mango juice in a medium bowl, add gelatin, let stand for about 1 minute, add rum and boiling water, stir gently for about 1 minute until the gelatin is completely dissolved. Let the mixture cool for about 15 minutes.

- Step 5: Pour the mango juice mixture over the cake surface through an inverted spoon so that the mixture evenly coats the surface of the cake. Then put the cake in the freezer for about 1 hour to be ready to use.

- If you don't use it right away, put it back in the fridge to keep it cold!

- Step 6: Before eating, remove the cake from the mold, inject fresh cream and decorate it with mint leaves or chopped mango pieces as you like.
- So even if you don't have an oven, you can still show off your skills in making great quality cakes for the whole family on the weekend!

Cherry cake

- Ingredients for making Cherry Cake
-
- Baking powder 120 gr
- Cherry 120 gr
- Heavy Cream 300 gr
- White Chocolate 50 gr
- Sugar 165 gr
- Unsalted Butter 40 gr

- Chicken eggs 4 eggs
- Honey 15 gr
- Fresh milk 55 gr
- Vanilla essence 5 gr
- Lemon juice 10 gr
- Gelatin 2 gr
- 1 little sugar syrup
- 1 little food coloring

- Implementation tools
- Oven, whisk, 18cm . round mold

- How to make Cherry Cake

- 1 Beat egg
- Place a bowl on a pot of hot water, then add 4 eggs, 100g of sugar, 15g of honey, 5g of vanilla essence and stir the mixture until it reaches nearly 40 degrees Celsius.
- Remove the bowl from the pot, use an electric mixer to beat the mixture until it turns white.
- After that, add a little white and red food coloring and continue to beat until the mixture is blended, lift the whisk to flow like a ribbon (Ribbon Stage State) is done.
- Pro tip: Warming the eggs will make them easier to fluff. However, you should only warm the eggs to about 40 - 50 degrees Celsius, otherwise the eggs will be overcooked and less fluffy.

- 2 Mix cake batter
- Sift 120g of cake flour into the egg yolk.
- Use a spatula to gently mix the mixture from bottom to top. Bring the spatula to the bottom of the bowl, lift the heavy ingredients, and fold aside. Continue until the mixture is combined.
- Heat the water bath to melt 35g unsalted butter and 55g fresh milk, then add a little cake flour and stir well.

- Pour the melted butter mixture into the cake batter and continue to fold it until blended.

- 3 Molding and baking
- Preheat oven to 170 degrees Celsius for 15 minutes.
- Line the wax paper and pour the cake batter into the mold, then bake for 40 minutes at 170 degrees Celsius.
- When the cake cools, cut off the brown layer on the top and bottom. Next, cut the cake into 3 pieces according to the size of the 15cm mold.

- 4 Cooking cherry syrup
- Cherry remove seeds and cut into small pieces.
- Put the pot on the stove, add the cherry meat, 40g of sugar and stir over low heat until the cherries are soft and the water is colored.
- Add 10g of lemon juice, stir until the mixture boils and then turn off the heat.
- Finally, filter the mixture through a sieve to get the syrup part.

- 5 Whipping fresh cream
- In a bowl, add 300g heavy cream, 25g sugar, a little bit of cooked cherry meat, then beat with an electric mixer on medium speed until stiff, lift the whisk to create a vertical peak.
- Tips for quick whipped cream:
- Use cold cream, at least 30% fat.
- Keep the bowl and beaters cool during the whipping process by placing them in a bowl of iced water. You should use a metal bowl.

- Or place the bowl and whisk in the freezer for at least 15 minutes before whipping.

- 6 Matching cakes
- Spread a little sugar syrup on the surface of a piece of cake, then cover with a layer of fresh cream about 1 inch high.
- Continue repeating these 2 coatings to the 3rd cake. At this point, you will cover the cake with fresh cream and then put it in the refrigerator.
- Heat 50g white chocolate, 5g unsalted butter, 2g soaked gelatin in water bath. Then, add 30g of cherry syrup, a little red food coloring and stir well.
- Strain the cherry syrup mixture through a sieve. Coat the cake evenly and then let the mixture flow around to create a dripping effect.

- 7 Finished Products
- Cherry cream cake is fragrant, greasy, fresh cream, fleshy from the core of the cake with the characteristic sweet and sour taste of cherry, delicious to eat without feeling bored!

Passion fruit tiramisu

- Ingredients

- Sugar 90 gr
- Wheat flour 60 gr
- Corn flour 40 gr
- Egg yolks 4 pieces
- Cooking oil 30 ml
- Passion fruit juice 40 ml
- Passion fruit oil 1 teaspoon

- Egg whites 4 pieces
- Salt 1/4 teaspoon
- Cream cheese 250 gr
- Ground sugar 70 gr
- Fresh milk cream 300 gr
- Passion fruit pulp 50 ml

- How to make passion fruit gato tiramisu cake

- 1 Mix cake batter
- Put in a bowl 20g granulated sugar, 60g flour, 40g cornstarch, mix well with a spatula, then add 4 egg yolks, 30ml cooking oil, 40ml passion fruit juice, 1 teaspoon passion fruit essential oil. , you use a spatula to stir until the mixture is smooth.

- 2 Beat egg whites
- In a bowl, add 4 egg whites, 1/4 teaspoon salt, beat with a hand mixer until the eggs bubble like soap bubbles, then slowly add 70g sugar and beat together.
- Beat until soft, lift the beater to see a peak.

- 3 Mix flour with egg whites
- Slowly scoop out the egg white cream mixed with the cake batter in step 1.
- Use a spoon to mix the flour, each time scooping a spoonful of egg white cream in the fold method (just gently stirring in one direction, pushing) to combine, then scoop the egg white cream again.
- Note:
- When mixing the ingredients, you should mix them very gently or fold them (mixing inversion and flipping from the bottom) and do not mix well to avoid breaking a lot of air bubbles that will not bloom well.
- If the flour mixture after mixing is too loose and there are many air bubbles, it may be due to improper mixing of the flour or inadequate egg-beating. This is the main cause of your sponge cake after baking cally

- 4 Molding and baking
- After mixing the dough, pour it into a round cake pan lined with non-stick parchment paper, spread the dough evenly and then lightly tap the mold a few times.
- Pre-heat oven at 160 degrees Celsius for 10 minutes to stabilize the temperature.
- Bake the cake at 150 C for 40 - 50 minutes, the cake is cooked.
- Tips for adjusting oven temperature:

- The baking temperature will vary depending on the oven. For ovens with a size of less than 30L, there will often be a difference in temperature. So you may need to lower the baking tray and bake at a lower temperature of about 150 -160 degrees Celsius (because the above heat for small ovens will often be high).
- To help prevent the cake from collapsing after baking, you need to understand the temperature of your oven. You can use an oven thermometer to help adjust the oven temperature or observe the cake for the first 10 minutes, if you see that the cake is golden quickly, the cake is rising quickly, you need to lower the heat and extend the baking time to help improve the condition of your cake. me.

- 5 Making cream cheese
- Put in a bowl 250g cream cheese, 70g sugar, beat with a whisk, then add 300g fresh milk cream, continue to beat until the mixture is smooth.

- 6 Pairing cakes
- After the cake is finished baking, you cut it into 3 circles.
- Put 1 slice on a clean plate, use a brush to soak the passion fruit syrup evenly on the cake. Next, scoop 1/3 of the cream cheese on top, use a spatula to smooth it out. Continue to place a piece of cake on top of the cream cheese layer and do the same for the rest of the ingredients.
- In the top layer of cheese, you put a thin layer of cream on the side of the cake, rotate and brush to make the cream even and beautiful.
- Place the cake in the refrigerator for 1 hour for the cream cheese to harden, then take the cake out, scoop out the passion fruit pulp to cover the cake and you're done.

- 7 Finished Products
- The cake is soft and smooth, blended with greasy cream cheese with the characteristic sweet and sour passion fruit. All make up the extremely delicious and attractive Gato tiramisu with passion fruit.
- Tips for successful implementation
- When whisking egg whites, to stabilize the air bubbles you should beat from low to high speed. If you beat the high speed at the beginning, the egg whites will become fluffy but also easily flattened.
- When mixing egg whites with cake flour, pay attention to mix slowly according to the folding method to help the cake become spongy, not cally, flattened.
- Matching the cake on the turntable helps to remove the ice cream easily, the cake is even and rounder.

PAVLOVA CAKE

MATERIALS:

- MERINGUE:
- Chicken eggs: 5 eggs
- Cream of tartar: 4 grams
- Sugar: 100 grams
- Icing sugar: 100 grams
- Salt: 3 grams
- Cornstarch: 5 grams
- PASSION SYRUP:
- Passion fruit juice: 200 ml (leave the seeds whole)
- Sugar: 100 grams
- Lemon juice: 5 ml
- ToppingWhipping cream: 30 ml
- A few strawberries and other sour fruits of your choice for garnish.

- HOW TO MAKE SWEET PAVLOVA:

- MAKE MERINGUE
- Step 1: Separate the yolk and white of the egg into two bowls. Then beat the egg whites with the cream of tartar.
- Step 2: Add 100 grams of sugar into the bowl in step 1, beat until the mixture is smooth, then stop.
- Step 3: Mix the mixture in step 2 with salt, cornstarch and remaining sugar evenly. When the mixture is smooth, place it in a triangle bag with an ice cream tip attached and shape it into a large rectangle or whatever shape you like on a baking tray lined with parchment paper. If you have leftover mixture, you can shape it into small spirals next to it.
- Step 4: Put the cake in the oven at 1200C for 40 minutes.

Strawberry pudding

MATERIALS:

- Whipping cream: 150g
- Strawberry: 300g
- Fresh milk: 200ml
- Sugar: 50g
- Gelatin leaves: 5 leaves

HOW TO MAKE A DELICIOUS Strawberry PUDDING:

- Step 1: Soak the gelatin leaves in fresh milk for about 15 minutes to soften the gelatin.

- Step 2: Put the fresh milk and gelatin, add the prepared sugar and whipping cream on the stove, simmer until the mixture dissolves, then turn off the heat.

- Step 3: Wash the strawberries, cut them into small pieces, then put them in a blender, then add them to the mixture in step 2. Gently stir the mixture until the mixture is evenly mixed.

- Step 4: Pour the mixture into a glass jar or cake mold as you like, let the mixture cool and then put it in the refrigerator for about 3 hours to freeze and enjoy.

Matcha Cream Cake

- Ingredients

- Eggs 155 gr
- Sugar 90 gr
- Honey 10 gr
- Vanilla extract 2 gr
- Unsalted Butter 40 gr
- Milk 45 gr
- Green tea powder 115 gr

- Sugar 45 gr
- Hot milk cream 20 gr
- White chocolate 60 gr
- Whipping Cream 250 gr (Fresh cream)
- Cake flour 95 gr
- Gelatin powder 2 gr (1 leaf gelatin foil)
- Cream Cheese 150 gr

- Fresh milk without sugar 45 gr
- Oven, egg beater, bowl, whisk, round mold with removable base 18cm in diameter,...

- How to make Matcha Green Tea Cake

- 1 Whip the whole egg
- Put 155g eggs, 90g sugar, 10g honey, 29g vanilla extract in a mixing bowl and beat the eggs. Put a pot of hot water below, a bowl of eggs on top (you should use a thick bowl to avoid overheating the eggs), the water below has a temperature of about 40 - 50 degrees Celsius. Beat until egg temperature About 40 degrees Celsius, take it out.
- Then use a whisk to beat the eggs until the eggs are thick, smooth, ivory white, and when you lift the beater, the mixture has a top.
- Note: The beaten eggs must be at room temperature, if the eggs are taken out of the refrigerator, let the eggs cool down first before performing this step.
- Beat the eggs one way and the eggs must be whipped, otherwise when mixing the dough, the air bubbles in the eggs will easily break and cause the cake to rise poorly.
- Warming the eggs helps them foam better, reduces large air bubbles, and helps stabilize the cake's structure.

- 2 Mix the dough
- Sift 95gr of cake flour and 10gr of green tea powder into the beaten eggs, then use a spatula to mix gently, scraping and scooping up from the bottom to avoid breaking the air bubbles so that the cake does not bloom beautifully.

- 3 Mix flour with butter
- Add 30g of melted unsalted butter, cooled to about 50-60 degrees Celsius, with 45g of unsweetened fresh milk, then use a mixer and mix well, then add a little of the above flour mixture and beat with an electric mixer. even.
- After the flour and butter have been mixed together, put in the remaining egg powder mixture, use a spatula to scrape and scoop from the bottom up for all the ingredients to blend together.

- 4 Molding and baking
- Turn on the oven at 170 degrees Celsius before 15 minutes to stabilize the temperature. Continue to put the cake into the 18cm diameter mold lined with parchment paper.
- Then slowly add the dough, hit the mold on the table to break up the large air bubbles, put the cake in the oven and bake at 170 degrees Celsius for 35 minutes.
- After baking, the cake must be left to cool completely before it can be decorated.

- 5 Make green tea cream cheese mixture
- In a bowl, mix 200g cream cheese and 45g sugar, use a beater to beat the mixture until soft, use a spatula and scraper to make the mixture more even, then sift 5g green tea powder in. Continue using the mixer and beat until combined. Then let cool to coat evenly.
- Add 250g of fresh milk cream to the mixture and use an electric mixer to beat until the mixture is soft and peaks. If you beat hard, the mixture will easily separate from water.
- Add 5g of green tea powder to 200g of hot milk cream and mix well with a spatula. Then place a cup of 60g white chocolate in a pot of hot water, melt the chocolate, then add 8g of unsalted butter with a little bit of green tea cheese mixture made, then add 2g of gelatin leaves, stir melt the mixture. Then wait for the mixture to warm slightly, then put it in the ice cream bag to make the coating

- 6 Decorate and finish the cake
- When the cake has cooled, use the green tea cheese mixture to evenly coat and smooth the cake, then put the cake in the refrigerator for 1 hour. Take out the cake and use the mixture in the icing bag to decorate and make the cake topping according to your preference!

- 7 Finished Products
- You can sprinkle matcha green tea powder on the cake according to your preference, garnish with green tea leaves. So you have finished the green tea cheese cake! The sweet and refreshing taste of green tea combined with the seductive cheese flavor will definitely become the go-to dish of green tea devotees!

- Tips for successful implementation and maintenance:

- Eggs used to make cakes must be fresh eggs, otherwise the eggs will be beaten poorly. The egg must be beaten properly or the cake will not bloom and easily smell.
- If the cake is left overnight to absorb moisture and get wet, just wait for the cake to dry and then wrap the cake in the freezer, when using you just need to defrost it to use it normally.
- You can replace whipping cream with butter cream or topping cream.
- Unused whipping cream can be kept in the refrigerator, wipe off the cream sticking to the mouth of the box, cover it with plastic wrap and then put it in the refrigerator, this way will preserve the Whipping cream for about half. month.
- To preserve cream cheese when using, you should use a clean knife or spoon to cut it, then cover the remaining unused cream cheese and put it in the refrigerator.

Flan

INGREDIENTS:

- Chicken eggs 4 eggs
- 1 chicken egg (yolk)
- Coconut milk 250 ml
- Fresh milk without sugar 450 ml
- Water 70 ml
- White sugar 220 gr
- Lemon juice 10 ml

INSTRUCTIONS:

- Step 1: Cooking caramel
- Put 140g of sugar and 70ml of water in a small pot and boil until the sugar turns the color of cockroach wings, then add 10ml of lemon juice, shake the pot with your hands to mix the lemon juice into the caramel and turn off the heat. Then pour the caramel into the prepared porcelain mold.

- Step 2: Heat the milk mixture
- Put 250ml of coconut milk and 450ml of unsweetened fresh milk in a small pot. Stir the mixture well and cook until there is a slight smoke, try the hot coconut milk, then turn off the heat.

- Step 3: Mix the ingredients
- Crack 4 eggs and 1 egg yolk into a mixing bowl. Put 80g of sugar in a bowl and beat gently with a whisk until the sugar is completely dissolved.
- Slowly pour the coconut milk into the egg and sugar bowl, stirring while pouring to combine the ingredients.

- Step 4: Bake
- Strain the flan mixture through a sieve. Then pour into each ceramic mold with caramel. Next, pour boiling water into the tray and put it in a water-bath oven at 170 degrees for about 20-25 minutes.

- Step 5: Finished product
- Place the cake on a plate and add some grated coconut to make the cake more beautiful. The delicious cake is rich in the fatty aroma of coconut milk, biting into the spreading flavor that makes you unable to stop.

Pineapple grilled cheese cake

INGREDIENTS:

- Flour No. 8 30 gr
- Unsalted Butter 18 gr
- Cream cheese 430 gr
- Pineapple 1 fruit
- Sugar 103 gr
- Yogurt without sugar 30 gr
- Chicken eggs 3
- Pineapple jam 1 piece
- Filtered water 50 ml

INSTRUCTIONS:

- Step 1: Preparing molds, preliminarily processing pineapples
- First, you use 2 pieces of foil to cover the 18cm removable base round mold. Then, wrap the wax paper on the inside of the mold and secure it with a stapler.
- Next, place this 12cm round mold in another larger round mold.
- Cut the two ends of the pineapple, then stand the pineapple upright and peel it from the top down. After removing the skin, wash the pineapple and drain it.

- Step 2: Pineapple shape
- First, lay the pineapple horizontally and then cut it into many circles about 1 inch thick, then use a small round hole to cut off the core.
- Next, arrange 4 pieces of pineapple on a baking tray, then sprinkle with a layer of powdered sugar and bake for 90 minutes at 90 degrees Celsius.
- Once baked, cut the pineapple into small triangular pieces.

- Step 3: Smooth cream cheese
- Finely grind 430gr Cream cheese, then add 30gr unsweetened yogurt and mix well.

- Step 4: Beat eggs and sifted flour

- Put 3 egg yolks, 38g sugar in a bowl and stir with a spatula until the mixture becomes fluffy, turns ivory white, and flows like a ribbon (Ribbon Stage).
- Next, sift into the bowl 30g flour and continue to stir until the mixture is smooth.

- Step 5: Mix the powder with pineapple juice
- Put the pot on the stove, add the pineapple juice and stir over medium heat until it boils. When the water boils, continue stirring for another 1-2 minutes, then turn off the heat.
- After cooking is complete, you weigh to get exactly 280g of pineapple juice.
- Next, pour the pineapple juice into the bowl of flour and stir well to combine.
- Put the mixture just stirred into the pot and continue to stir over low heat until it sets a thick consistency.
- Then, add 18g unsalted butter and stir once more.
- Finally, filter the mixture through a sieve into the bowl of cream cheese, add 10ml of lemon juice, mix well.

- Step 6: Mix flour and egg whites
- Place 3 egg whites in a new bowl and beat on low speed with an electric mixer until foamy.
- Divide 65g of sugar into 3 parts, slowly add each part and beat until dissolved.

- Beat each sugar for about 30 seconds on low speed, then add the next sugar to beat.
- When adding the last sugar to the eggs, turn on the mixer at high speed, beat the eggs until When the eggs are soft, creamy, the mixture is flexible, glossy and smooth. Lift the spatula to create a standing top, but swing it down and you're done.
- Bring the spatula to the bottom of the bowl, lift the heavy ingredients, and fold aside. Continue until the mixture is combined.

- Step 7: Molding, baking
- Preheat oven to 170 degrees Celsius for 15 minutes.
- First, you pour the flour mixture into a small mold, then arrange the grilled pineapple pieces on top of the dough.
- Place 2 molds in the baking tray, pour boiling water on the tray and bake for 30 minutes at 160 degrees Celsius.
- After the cake is cooked, let it cool completely and spread a layer of pineapple jam on top to enjoy.

- Step 8: Finished product
- Pineapple cheese cake just out of the oven is already full of aroma, the cake core is super soft, moist, smooth with a little bit of fat from cream cheese, served with grilled pineapple topping, extremely delicious.

CREAM BRULEE

INGREDIENTS:

- 6 chicken eggs
- 400ml whipping cream
- 3ml vanilla
- 40g sugar
- A little salt
- 3g sugar for caramel (per 1 cake)

HOW TO MAKE CREAM BRULEE AT HOME

- MAKE POWDER
- Put egg yolks in a bowl, add sugar and salt to a large bowl, mix the mixture together with a whisk. You should note at this stage that you need to beat the eggs evenly in one direction until the sugar and salt are completely dissolved and the eggs turn light.
- Put whipping cream in a saucepan and boil over low heat until the cream is slightly warm (about 70 degrees Celsius). Then we add this mixture with the egg yolks made in the above step, just pour in and stir until the mixture blends together. Add vanilla and stir once more.
- Sift the two mixtures that have just been made to be smooth and remove clumps, this helps you when making the cake to have a smoother surface. After sifting all the mixture, remove all the foam.

- PREPARATION OF CAKE
- Prepare a ceramic cake pan, then pour this mixture into about ¾ of the cake pan. Do the same until you run out of dough.

- BAKEDING STAGE
- Prepare a baking tray, add hot water about 2/3 of the cake tray and then place the cake mold in. Bring the cake tray to bake in the oven at a temperature of about 150 degrees Celsius for 30-45 minutes until the cake in the mold shakes slightly, the cake is ready.

- COMPLETE AND ENJOY
- After baking, take it out of the baking tray, let it cool down, then take it out and enjoy. When eating, you will perform the torch process.
- When enjoying, you sprinkle a thin layer of sugar on top of the cake to make the caramel part, then use a torch to burn directly on the surface of the cake until the sugar layer melts and turns dark brown. The sugar hardens a bit and you can enjoy it.

Mango mousse

INGREDIENTS:

- Cake base:
- 80g biscuits
- 35g room temperature unsalted butter
- Mousse:
- 250ml whipping cream
- 50g sugar
- 15g gelatin
- 250g mango meat
- Mango side:
- 4g gelatin
- 120g mango meat

INSTRUCTIONS:

- Step 1: Heat butter in a water bath or microwave until melted. Put the biscuits in a blender until smooth, then mix with the butter until smooth. Using a removable cake pan, pour cookies into it and press it down to beat the mold. Then put it in the fridge for 30 minutes to harden.

- Step 2: Make the mango mousse, put the mango with 2 tablespoons water and sugar in a blender and puree.

- Step 3: Soak the gelatin in water until soft, then add a little water and boil in a water bath to dissolve the gelatin. Whipped fresh cream, then pour the pureed mango and gelatin into the mix.

- Step 4: Pour the mango cream into the cake pan, flatten it. Then refrigerate for at least 4 hours for the mango mousse to solidify.

- Step 5: To make the mango layer, put 70ml of water with gelatin in a water bath to melt the gelatin. Put the mango in a blender and blend it with the gelatin. Wait for the mango mousse to freeze, then slowly pour this mango layer on your face, you can add more mango pieces on top to increase the flavor of the cake.

Black Forest ice cream cake

INGREDIENTS:

- 9 eggs
- Cake flour 200 gr
- Fresh milk without sugar 80 ml
- Cooking oil 60 ml
- Cocoa powder 30 gr
- Canned black cherries 1 box
- Fresh black cherries 200 gr
- Cherry Brandy 10 ml
- Whipping cream 500 gr
- Ground sugar 40 gr
- Chocolate 50 gr
- (cocoa content from 10-35%)
- Salt 3 gr
- Ground sugar 40 gr
- White granulated sugar 150 gr

INSTRUCTIONS:

- Step 1: Mix the dough to make the cake core
- Put 9 eggs, 3g salt and 150g sugar in a mixing bowl and beat the eggs. Put a pot of hot water below, a bowl of eggs on top (should use a thick bowl to avoid overheating, causing the eggs to cook), the water below has a temperature of about 40 - 50 degrees Celsius.
- Beat the eggs until the eggs are thick, smooth, ivory-white, and when you lift the whisk, the eggs will flow like a ribbon.
- Add 200g of sifted Cake flour and gently mix the mixture with a spatula, then add 80ml of unsweetened fresh milk and gently mix the mixture.
- Mix 60ml of cooking oil and 3g of cocoa together and then slowly add it to the prepared cake flour mixture, then gently mix.
- Note: The beaten eggs must be at room temperature, if the eggs are taken from the refrigerator, let the eggs cool down first before doing this step. Beat the eggs one way and the eggs must be whipped, otherwise when mixing the dough, the air bubbles in the eggs will easily break and cause the cake to rise poorly.
- When mixing the ingredients, you should mix them very gently or fold them (mixing inversion and flipping from the bottom) and do not mix well to avoid breaking a lot of air bubbles that will not bloom well.

- Step 2: Bake
- Turn on the oven at 180 degrees Celsius before about 10-15 minutes for the temperature to stabilize. Place the dough into a round pan lined with parchment paper, gently tap the pan on the table to break up large air bubbles, then place in the oven for 25 minutes.
- When the cake is done, turn the mold upside down and remove the cake to let it cool completely on a rack.

- Step 3: Making the cake
- Use a blender to grind 100g of canned cherries. Cook the crushed cherry with 150ml of cherry juice and 30g of sugar and 10g of cornstarch, stir until the mixture is completely dissolved, add 10ml of Cherry Brandy, stir well, then turn off the heat, let it cool.

- Step 4: Whipping cream
- Whip 500g Whipping cream with 40g powdered sugar. Beat until stiff peaks form.
- Note: Whipping cream must be cold to whip, so put the whipping cream in the refrigerator 30-60 minutes before whipping.

- Step 5: Cake decoration
- Take a portion of the pie crust, spread the filling evenly over the cake with a brush, and then add some whipped cream and a few canned cherries. Use another layer of cake on top and then do the same steps.

- Finally, add another layer of cake and garnish with fresh cherries and chopped chocolate on top. So we have completed a 3-tier black forest cake.
- Note: Allow the cake to cool completely before decorating to avoid melting the cream.

- Step 6: Finished product
- Black Forest cake is fragrant with the aroma of black cherry and typical Cherry Brandy combined with the slightly bitter taste of chocolate cake and greasy fresh cream all make a wonderful cake. This is a beautiful and attractive cake that is suitable for family parties.

TIRAMISU GREEN TEA

MATERIALS:

- Cake core:
- Chicken eggs: 2 (separate yolk and white)
- Sugar: 25 grams
- Vegetable oil: 30 grams
- Fresh milk without sugar: 45 grams
- All-purpose flour: 45 grams
- Corn flour: 10 grams Green tea powder: 5 grams
- Cream of tartar: 1/4 teaspoon
- Sugar: 20 grams
- Salt: a small pinch
- Part mascarpone

- Vanilla: 1/2 teaspoon
- Green tea powder: 10 grams
- Fine granulated sugar: 45 grams
- Mascarpone cheese (room temperature): 250 grams
- Fresh cream with 35% - 40% fat content (cold): 200ml
- Toppings:
- Honey: 1 tablespoon
- Green tea powder: 2-3 grams
- Fresh milk without sugar: 25 - 30 ml

HOW TO MAKE GREEN TEA TIRAMISU:

- MAKING THE GREEN TEA CAKE
- Preheat oven to 175 degrees Celsius, two fires. Line the bottom of the mold with parchment paper.
- Place the egg yolks and sugar in a bowl, and gently stir with a whisk to combine the eggs and sugar. Then, pour cooking oil and fresh milk into the egg bowl, stir well. Finally, sift flour, green tea powder and cornstarch into a bowl, continue to mix with a whisk until a homogeneous mixture is obtained.
- Beat egg whites with salt, cream of tartar and sugar until egg whites are frothy, lift a beater until peaks form.
- Add 1/3 of the egg whites to the yolk mixture and mix well. Continue doing this until you run out of whites.

- Pour the batter into the baking pan and shake gently to evenly distribute the dough. Bake the cake at 175 degrees C for 12 - 15 minutes or until the edge of the cake is slightly golden brown, gently press the surface of the cake to see the indentation immediately swell again.
- Remove the cake from the oven and separate from the mold. Peel off the paper at the bottom of the cake. Let the cake cool completely on a rack.

- MAKE MASCARPONE
- Place mascarpone, vanilla and green tea powder in a bowl. Beat at the lowest speed for about 60 – 90 seconds.
- Put the sugar in a bowl of fresh cream, stir well. Pour this whipped cream and sugar into the green tea mascarpone bowl and beat on medium speed until creamy. Note: Do not let the mixture be too thick and avoid beating for a long time to cause the cream to separate (the phenomenon is that the cream is no longer smooth but messy and lumpy).
- Pour the cream mixture into a clean bowl and refrigerate for 20-30 minutes.

- FINISHING THE FINISHED PRODUCTS
- Heat milk and honey, stir well until the honey dissolves.

- Divide the pie crust into 3 parts – cut horizontally. Next, use a brush to spread a layer of honey milk on the cake and then spread 1/3 of the Tiramisu green tea cream on it. Place the 2nd cake layer, repeat the steps of spreading milk and cream. Put the 3rd cake layer, spread the honey milk, spread the remaining cream on the face.
- Once done, leave the cake in the refrigerator for another 4-6 hours to thicken the Tiramisu and moisten the cake core.

- ENJOY
- When enjoying, use a sharp knife to cut the cake into bite-sized pieces. Each time you cut, wipe the knife clean with a towel and sprinkle some green tea powder to decorate the finished product more eye-catching. It is recommended to serve the cake with a drink of your choice to enhance the taste.

MACARON

MATERIALS:

- Cake dough part
- 80 grams of butter, 150 grams icing sugar
- 150 grams of almond powder
- 110 grams of egg whites
- 150 grams of white granulated sugar
- 400ml whipping cream
- The crust part, 40ml water
- 150 grams of white granulated sugar
- 110 grams of egg whites
- A little food coloring
- Cake filling
- 40 grams of butter
- 100 grams of strawberry jam
- 100 grams of blueberry jam
- 600 grams of white chocolate
- 200 grams of black chocolate
- 200ml whipping cream

INSTRUCTIONS:

- POWDER MIXING:
- Puree the almond flour and icing sugar in a blender and strain the mixture through a sieve.
- Place the whipping cream and butter in a bowl, use the water bath method to melt the butter and stir well to combine the two ingredients.
- White chocolate and dark chocolate are also boiled in a water bath to melt. The heating process needs to be stirred continuously so that the chocolate does not burn.
- Puree almond flour and icing sugar

- MAKING THE CAKE:
- Put the pot on the stove, add sugar and water and bring to a boil to 180 degrees C. Then, beat 50 grams of egg whites with a whisk, then pour in the sugar water while whisking.
- Add a bit of food coloring to the crust mixture, beat until the mixture is evenly and beautifully colored.
- Mix the remaining egg whites with the prepared almond flour mixture, then add the crust mixture, continuing to mix gently until a homogeneous, smooth paste is obtained.
- Mix enough color for the cake to have a beautiful color

- Shaping and Baking CAKES:
- Put the cake mixture into the triangle bag that has a pre-installed icing tail.
- Line a baking tray with parchment paper, and skillfully shape the dough into small, even circles.
- Preheat the oven to 150 degrees Celsius for 10 minutes, then put the cake tray in the oven for about 12 minutes.

- How to make mini macarons:
- Make sure the oven temperature is right for the cake to rise evenly

- MAKING THE CAKE
- Put half of the butter and 100ml of whipping cream in a bowl, heat the water until the butter is completely melted.
- Pour the butter mixture into the bowl of the white chocolate, stir well to get the white ganache filling. Then, take 1/3 white ganache and mix with strawberry jam to make strawberry ganache. Continue to take 1/3 of white ganache to mix with blueberry jam to get blurberry ganache.
- Heat the remaining butter and whipping cream in a water bath, then pour into a bowl of dark chocolate, mix well to finish the dark ganache filling.

WAFFLE CAKE

INGREDIENTS FOR WAFFLE:

- 140 grams of baking powder
- 110 grams of white granulated sugar
- 3 chicken eggs
- 120 grams of butter
- Vanilla
- Salt
- Sugar

IMPLEMENTATION STEPS:

- MIXING FOR EGGS
- Put the butter in the microwave for 40-50 seconds to completely melt the butter. If you don't have a microwave, you can melt the butter by heating it in a pan.
- Separate the egg yolks and egg whites into two separate bowls. Next, pour 55 grams into the yolk bowl, beat well, then add another 100 grams of melted butter, continue to beat until the ingredients blend together into a homogeneous mixture.

- WAFFLE DRY MIXING
- Put the remaining sugar in the bowl of the egg whites, beat until fluffy. Then pour the egg white mixture into the yolk mixture bowl, mix well from bottom to top until the mixture is smooth and has an eye-catching light yellow color.
- Sift the flour through once to make the flour very smooth, then add the yolk mixture with a little salt and vanilla, mix well to make the mixture smooth and without lumps.

- HOW TO BAKE WAFFLE
- Heat a waffle maker, spread butter on both sides of the cake. When you see that the mold is ready, slowly pour in the cake flour mixture, spreading it evenly.

- Close the machine and bake for about 5 minutes or wait until the cake turns golden brown, then remove from the mold. Use a knife to cut off the excess around, arrange the cake on a plate. Continue to repeat the baking operation until all of the prepared dough is used up.

- ENJOY
- Cut the cake into nice small pieces, sprinkle powdered sugar on top and enjoy. You can also add fruit and ice cream to enhance the flavor of the waffle and eat it without getting bored.

Colorful birthday pancakes

MATERIALS:

- M: tablespoon - m: teaspoon
- pre-mixed doughnuts 2 packs
- Color for 35g
- Green tea color 35g
- Gac color 35g
- Topping cream 200g
- Powdered sugar 1m
- Served with: basil, raspberries

- PREPARED:

- Make cake decorating cream: Put the 50% defrosted cream topping in a bowl, beat with an electric mixer until soft, put the cream in a triangle bag to catch whipped cream, keep it cold.
- Mixing gardenia: mix 2 gardenia seeds with 50ml of hot water
- Mix gac color: 1 tablespoon of gac fruit with a little white wine, a little cooking oil, 2/3 cup of water
- Mix green tea color: 1-2g green tea powder with 50ml warm water
- Mix dough: Put in 3 bowls, each bowl 50g Traditional pre-mixed donut flour with 35g colored water of each type.

- IMPLEMENTATION:
- Make a cake: Put a non-stick pan on the stove to heat, place on a pile of wet towels to let the pan cool down, then return to the stove, reduce the heat, use a spatula to pour the batter into the center of the pan, fry the cake to make small bubbles and rim the cake. Once it is closed, use a plastic stone to turn the cake over, fry for another 30 seconds until the cake is cooked, take out a plate. Then, turn the cake with the remaining 2 colors.

- HOW TO USE:
- Place 1 pancake on a plate, top with cream topping, place 1 more cake, decorate all 3 layers of cake in turn, decorate the top with cream, sprinkle with powdered sugar and birthday decorations.

Blueberry yogurt mousse

- Ingredients for making blueberry yogurt mousse

- Blueberry jam 152 gr
- Cornstarch 10 gr (corn flour)
- Whipping cream 150 ml
- 2 eggs
- Fresh milk 7 ml
- Yogurt 100 gr (unsweetened)

- Vanilla extract 1/4 teaspoon
- Almond powder 10 gr
- Gelatin 5 leaves
- All-purpose flour 20 gr
- Cooking oil 13 gr
- Sugar 50 gr
- 1 pinch salt

- Implementation tools
- Oven, whisk, sieve

- How to make Blueberry Yogurt Mousse Cake

- 1 Beat eggs
- In a bowl, add 2 egg whites, 1 pinch of salt and beat with a hand mixer, add a few 1/4 teaspoons of cream of tartar and beat until foamy.
- Divide 40g of sugar into 3 parts, add each part and beat until dissolved. Beat each sugar for about 30 seconds on low speed, then add the next sugar to beat.
- When adding the last sugar to the eggs, turn on the mixer at high speed, beat the eggs until the eggs are soft, creamy, the mixture is flexible, glossy and smooth, lift the whisk to create a soft peak, turn it down to achieve.
- Slowly add the beaten egg yolks to the egg whites, using a mixer until well combined.
- In a bowl, add 13g of cooking oil, 7g of unsweetened milk and 1/4 teaspoon of vanilla essence and mix well.

- Continue slowly adding the milk mixture to the eggs, using the mixer on low speed.
- Pro tip: divide the sugar out into 2 or 3 parts and add it in little by little. Avoid putting in all at once.
- When beaten, the egg whites must be at room temperature (if taken from the refrigerator). Also you need to make sure the whites are free of impurities or other fats as this will prevent the eggs from forming.
- You can beat the eggs at 50 degrees Celsius to make the eggs faster and more stable.

- 2 Sift flour
- Mix 20g flour, 10g cornstarch and 10g almond flour together.
- Divide the dough into 2 parts, sift each part of the flour mixture into the egg mixture, use a patch to mix the dough, fold the mix by scooping and flipping from the bottom up to avoid breaking the air bubbles so that the cake does not bloom beautifully.
- Mix until the mixture is combined. Do the same with the rest of the dough.

- 3 Bake a cake
- Preheat the oven to 170 degrees Celsius for 15 minutes before baking to allow the oven to stabilize.
- Put the cake into a 16cm x 16cm cake pan, gently tap the cake mold on the table to remove large air bubbles.
- Put the cake in the oven, bake the cake at a temperature of 155 - 160 degrees Celsius for 30 minutes.

- Take the cake out, turn the cake pan upside down on the table to cool completely. Then use a knife to cut around the cake mold and remove the cake.
- Use a round mold to shape the cake.

- 4 Beat whipping cream
- Put in a bowl 150ml whipping cream (fat content from 30-40%), use a whisk to beat until the whipping cream is soft.
- Tip: After whipping the whipping cream is done, put it in the refrigerator to keep the whipping cream to mix the cream.

- 5 Make blueberry yoghurt mix and make mousse
- Put 3 gelatin leaves soaked in water.
- Heat 112g of blueberry jam with 10g of sugar on the stove, stirring until the sugar dissolves and the mixture is slightly warm.
- Put 3 gelatin leaves in a pot of blueberry jam that have been soaked and squeezed out of water, boil over low heat and stir quickly so that the gelatin is completely dissolved.
- When the gelatin has dissolved, turn off the heat and put the mixture in a bowl, add 100g of unsweetened yogurt and mix well. Divide the mixture into 2 parts.
- Slowly add the blueberry yoghurt mixture part by part to the previously whipped whipping cream and fold in a fold until the mixture is even and smooth.
- Pro tip: You can buy blueberry jam in stores or supermarkets without having to make your own jam with fresh fruit.

- 6 Make mousse
- Put a layer of blueberry yogurt cream in a glass, then add a layer of cake and continue to be a layer of blueberry yogurt cream on top. Place in the fridge for about 2 hours to set.

- Soak the remaining 2 gelatin leaves in water until the gelatin is soft. Put in the pot 30gr of blueberry jam and 60gr of hot water, Add the gelatin and stir quickly until the gelatin dissolves into the jam mixture.
- Take out the frozen mousse and put blueberry jelly on top, continue to put in the refrigerator for about 1 hour for the jelly to solidify.

- 7 Finished Products
- Garnish with some whipped cream and some blueberries, and you're done with the blueberry mousse.
- Layer by layer of cake, layer of delicious blueberry jelly, soft min, fatty leopard. This is a great idea for hot days.

Coconut cake

Materials:

- 100g corn flour
- 120g sugar
- 200ml coconut milk
- 2 eggs
- 500ml fresh milk without sugar
- Roasted black sesame then finely ground
- Finely ground roasted peanuts

INSTRUCTIONS:

- Step 1: In a large bowl, mix the cornstarch and 300ml fresh milk.

- Step 2: Put the remaining milk, coconut milk, and sugar in the pot. Heat the milk mixture over low heat until the sugar has dissolved.

- Step 3: Then add the mixed milk and flour, stirring while pouring. Cook over medium heat until mixture thickens and boils.

- Step 4: Prepare a square tray lined with food wrap. Then pour the cooked coconut cake batter into the mold and spread it thinly. Then wait for the mixture to cool, then put it in the refrigerator for about 1 hour.

- Step 5: When the coconut cake has cooled, cut it into equal sized squares.

- Step 6: Roll the coconut cake over the sesame and peanuts so that the cake is evenly coated. Coconut cake is smooth and cool, chewy and fatty, and the outside is covered with sesame or roasted peanuts, which are very attractive. This is sure to be a snack the whole family will love.

Orange grapefruit cream cake

- Ingredients

- Eggs 155 gr
- Sugar 90 gr
- Honey 10 gr
- Vanilla Essence 2 gr
- Unsalted butter 30 gr
- Fresh milk 45 gr
- Cake Flour 100 gr
- Orange peel 10 gr
- Yogurt 70 gr

- Honey 20 gr
- Orange peel 10 gr
- Whipping Cream 300 gr
- Sugar 30 gr
- Unsalted butter 5 gr
- White Chocolate 50 gr
- Grapefruit juice 30 gr
- Gelatin 2 gr

- White Chocolate 50 gr
- Unsalted butter 5 gr
- Orange juice 30 gr
- Gelatin 2 gr

- Implementation tools
- Bowl, stirrup, oven, cake mold,...

- How to make Orange Grapefruit Cake

- 1 Beat eggs whole
- Put in a bowl 155g eggs, 90g sugar, 10g honey, 2g vanilla essence and beat the eggs in a water bath. Place the bowl of eggs over the pot of hot water, then beat the eggs until smooth, the mixture reaches about 40 degrees Celsius, then remove the bowl from the pot.
- Use a mixer to beat the mixture from high speed to low speed (about 2 minutes each) until the mixture turns ivory white, thick, smooth and when lifting the whisk, the eggs melt like ribbons. is achieved.
- Note: Do not let the bottom of the bowl touch the water when stirring the mixture.
- Use a thick bowl to avoid overheating the eggs. The water below must have a temperature of about 40 - 50 degrees Celsius.

- 2 Mix the dough
- Sift 100g Cake Flour into the egg mixture.

- Use a spatula to gently mix from bottom to top. Bring the spatula to the bottom of the bowl, lift the heavy ingredients, and fold aside. Continue repeating until the mixture is smooth.

- Note: It is necessary to mix gently and correctly to avoid breaking air bubbles.

- 3 Mix butter
- Heat water bath 30g unsalted butter, 45g fresh milk. Add part of the flour mixture to the butter and milk mixture, then stir well.
- Pour the mixture back into the egg mixture and fold in a fold.
- Finally, add some grated orange peel and mix gently one more time.

- 4 Molding and baking
- Preheat oven to 180 degrees Celsius for 20 minutes.
- Pour the dough into the cake pan and bake at 170 degrees Celsius for 35 minutes.
- Note: You should spread the dough evenly and hit the mold on the table to break up large air bubbles.

- 5 Cut the cake
- After the cake has cooled completely, cut the cake into pieces about 1.5cm thick.

- 6 Cut oranges and grapefruits
- Peel the oranges and cut them into small pieces. Peel grapefruit, filter the pulp and remove only the flesh.

- 7 Making yogurt filling
- Put in a glass 70g yogurt, 20g honey, some orange peel and stir well.

- 8 Whipping whipping cream
- You put 300g Whipping Cream, 30g sugar in a new bowl, beat the mixture with a whisk until the cream is stiff, achieves a thick, smooth and clear texture, lift the spatula to create a vertical tip.

- Tip for quick whipped cream: Before whipping, put the ice cream in the fridge for 15 minutes, or you can put the bowl of ice cream in a bowl of ice water, then whip it.

- 9 Arrange the cake
- Spread a thin layer of yogurt over the cake, spread a layer of whipped whipping cream, and then add sliced oranges and grapefruits on top.
- Continue to cover the fruit with a thick layer of whipped cream.
- Add another layer of cake and moisten with the yogurt mixture.
- Add a thin layer of whipped cream, then a layer of fruit. Cover with thick whipped cream, add the last slice of cake and continue to moisten with remaining yogurt mixture.
- Note: Let the cake core cool completely before arranging the cake because hot cake will melt

- 10 Create toppings and cake decorations
- Cover the entire cake with whipped cream, then place in the fridge to firm up.
- Cut an orange in half, squeeze out the juice and strain it through a sieve to remove the fleshy cloves. Then you do the same with grapefruit.
- Melt 2 parts white chocolate and unsalted butter in a saucepan of hot water.
- Add the warmed orange juice, 2 soaked gelatin leaves, and a little food coloring to the chocolate and butter mixture, then stir well. Do the same with the grapefruit part.
- Put the 2 mixtures into the icing bag, cover the cake in turn in a drip effect.
- Next, add some fresh cream and garnish with sliced orange grapefruit and you're done.

- Note: orange and grapefruit juice can be warmed in the microwave.
- Let the mixture cool down to about 28 - 30 degrees Celsius before using.

- 11 Finished Products
- Eye-catching cream cake with colorful colors, blended with delicious layers. The first is a layer of greasy cream to a soft, smooth cake, adding a little sweetness and sourness from fruit. All create a strange and attractive cake.

- Tips for successful implementation:
- Do not beat the whipping cream for too long as it will cause the cream to separate from the water.

- If you don't have a removable mold, you should line a layer of wax paper or butter in the mold so that the finished product does not stick to the mold and is more beautiful.
- When the cake is cooked, do not take the cake out of the oven quickly because it will cause the cake to collapse due to thermal shock. At this point, you should turn off the oven and slightly open the oven, leave the cake in the oven for another 10 minutes before taking it out.
- Store the cake in the refrigerator and use it up to 3-4 days to keep its delicious taste.

Fruit cake

- Ingredients for making fruit cake

- Chicken eggs 4 eggs
- Sugar 100 g
- Vanilla tube 5 ml
- Honey 25 g
- Salt 1/2 teaspoon
- Unsalted Butter 40 g
- Fresh milk without sugar 40 g

- Cake flour 125 g
- White Chocolate 80g
- Whipping Cream 500 g
- Condensed milk 20g
- Strawberries 20 fruits
- Kiwi 3 fruits
- 1 mango

- How to make Fruit Cake

- 1 Beat egg mixture
- Put in a mixing bowl 4 eggs, 100g sugar, 1/2 teaspoon salt, 5ml vanilla essence, 25g honey. Use a hand whisk to stir until the egg mixture is melted and the ingredients are well combined.
- You prepare a pot of hot water, place the bowl on the pot to avoid touching the water. Continue to use a spatula to stir until the mixture is smooth and uniform. When white foam appears and the mixture reaches 40-41 degrees Celsius, remind the bowl to put it down on the table.
- Using a whisk, continue to beat the egg bowl with medium speed and gradually increase until the mixture turns ivory, the capacity in the bowl also increases, the cream is light, then turn off the machine.

- Note: Warming the eggs not only helps the sugar in the eggs dissolve faster, but also helps the egg mixture to swell faster and keep a stable structure when baking than not warming the eggs.
- Before you beat the eggs, you need to let them come to room temperature to avoid helping the mixture to become fluffy.
- Should use a bowl with a thick heart to avoid overheating the eggs and cook the eggs, at this time the eggs will be no or less fluffy.

- 2 Mix the flour mixture
- Pour the hot water into the tray, put the unsalted butter and 40ml fresh milk into the water bath until the butter melts and the milk warms up.

- Pour into the mixture 40ml of heated milk, use a spatula to stir until the powder is diluted.
- Sift through 100g of cake flour into the cake flour mixture, then use a spatula to mix well, sift another 25g of baking powder and continue stirring until the mixture is smooth. Then use a flat spatula to stir the mixture from the bottom up until no more coarse flour is visible.
- Use a spatula to scoop part of the flour mixture into the butter cup, stirring to loosen the butter mixture. This makes it easier to mix the flour with the butter than it is to add the butter directly to the flour mixture.
- After the butter mixture is smooth, add it to the flour bowl. Continue to use a flat spatula to gently stir the flour mixture from the bottom to the top. Do not stir vigorously will cause the dough mixture to separate and spoil. When the mixture is even, smooth and uniform, you stop.

- Note: Gently stir the dough from the bottom up, avoid stirring too hard, which will break many air bubbles in the cake, making it difficult for the cake to rise.

- 3 Bake the sponge cake
- Preheat oven to 170 degrees Celsius for 15 minutes to stabilize oven temperature.
- You prepare a cake mold lined with parchment paper and pour the dough in, spreading it evenly throughout the mold. Gently tap the pan on the table to break up the large air bubbles inside the dough

- 4 Preliminary processing of fruit
- Strawberries are washed, use a knife to cut off the petioles, cut half of the strawberries into thin slices, and cut the rest into quarters for decoration.
- Kiwi is washed, cut off the first two parts, use a spoon to "plug" around the inside of the fruit to remove the peel. Divide the kiwi into two parts, one cut into round slices, the other cut each piece in half into two halves.
- Cut the mango in half, use the tip of a knife to cut it into vertical lines, then use a spoon to scoop out the cut meat. Similar to strawberries and kiwi cut half into thin slices for filling, half cut into longitudinal lines.
- Put the fruit for garnish and the fruit for the filling on a separate plate.
- Tip: Using a spoon to peel the skin helps to separate the shell thinly, does not consume a lot of meat, helps to keep the shape of the fruit, limiting the knife cutting into the hand while peeling.

- 5 Cut the cake
- When the cake is done, bring out the cake, remove the parchment paper and place the cake on a rack, let the cake cool completely, then cut and decorate the cake.
- After the cake has cooled completely, cut the cake into 4 equal pieces about 1cm thick.
- Tip: In order not to waste time, you can make the cake core 1 day before and use it the next day.

- 6 Making ice cream
- Put the pot on the stove, low heat. Pour 80g whipping cream into the pot, stir gently until the milk is hot, then turn off the heat, lower the pot.
- Pour the warmed milk cream into 80g white chocolate, use a spatula to mix until the chocolate melts evenly. Add 25g of sugar and stir until the sugar dissolves, then add 20g of condensed milk and stir well.
- Pour some ice into a separate bowl then place the chocolate bowl on top. Place in a mixing bowl 350g cold whipping cream, beat on medium speed with an electric mixer until the cream thickens, then remove the bowl from the ice bowl.
- Pour the cream into a small bowl, keep 200g of cream in the bowl, put the small bowl in the refrigerator. Continue using the mixer to beat from low speed to high speed until the cream is stiff, with a clear creamy texture, lift the whisk to create a vertical flash.
- Note: When the mixture is too hot, don't let the condensed milk stir immediately, but wait for the mixture to cool down, then add condensed milk and stir.

- 7 Making fruit cake
- Take out the first layer of cake, use a spatula to brush the sugar water on top of the cake, put the fresh cream on it, then use a knife to smooth it, then cover the cut strawberries and then add a layer of fresh cream to cover the strawberry layer. , continue to use the knife to smooth.

- Take the second layer of cake on top, use a knife to smooth the fresh cream, then put the mango filling on top and spread the cream evenly to cover the mango.
- Similar to the 3rd cake layer, also give a layer of cream, then a layer of kiwi and then a layer of cream.
- Finally, put the 4th layer of cake on and use fresh cream to cover it and rub it all over.
- Put the ice cream in the refrigerator into a triangle bag, put the cream on the top to decorate, then put the fruit on the middle of the cake, sprinkle with a little powdered sugar or decorate with flowers to make the cake look eye-catching.

- 8 Finished Products
- Biting a piece of cake, you will feel the sweet and sour taste from the fresh fruits combined with the soft layer of the cake and the fragrant fresh cream. It all comes together to make a wonderful cake.

BUTTERFLY CAKES

MATERIALS:

- Chicken eggs: 4 eggs
- Yellow sugar: 300 grams
- Unsalted butter: 300 grams
- Self-raising flour: 300 grams
- SIZE SECTION
- Yellow sugar: 300 grams
- Vanilla Extract
- Water: 300ml
- BUTTER CREAM PART
- Unsalted butter: 400 grams
- Ground sugar: 550 grams
- DECORATION SECTION
- Strawberry
- Cookie
- Mashed chocolate

HOW TO MAKE BEAUTIFUL BUTTERFLY CAKES:

- MAKE THE CAKE OF THE CAKE
- In turn, put all the ingredients for the prepared cake into the bowl, use a whisk to beat until the mixture is homogeneous and turns light yellow.
- Carefully pour the batter into the Cupcake mold. Then, preheat the oven at 180 degrees C for 10 minutes and then put the cake in the oven for 10 to 15 minutes.
- When the time is up, poke a toothpick in the center of the cake. If the toothpick doesn't stick to the dough, it means the cake is done, if the toothpick is wet, bake the cake for a few more minutes
- Making syrup
- Put a small pot on the stove, add sugar, water and vanilla, stir well and boil for 2-3 minutes.
- Wait for the syrup to cool completely, filter through a sieve to remove any residue.

- MAKING BUTTER CREAM
- Mix butter with powdered sugar and 100ml syrup. Next, beat the butter mixture with an electric mixer until smooth and even.
- Place buttercream in a piping bag.

- DECORATE
- Take out the Cupcakes, use a knife to cut 1 shallow circle from each cake, then cut the round cake in half to create a butterfly shape.
- Cover the cake with buttercream, decorate with strawberries and cake according to your preferences to complete the Butterfly cakes.

- FINISHED PRODUCTS REQUEST
- Butterfly cakes not only look like beautiful butterfly wings but also taste very delicious and attractive. The soft, moist cake is blended with greasy butter cream, adding a little fresh fruit flavor that anyone can't refuse.

Yogurt cake

INGREDIENTS:

- 200ml yogurt
- 50g flour
- 2 eggs
- 5g sugar
- Some raisins, orange juice, some salt.

INSTRUCTIONS:

- Put flour in a bowl, add salt, sugar and beat eggs.
- Making smooth, creamy yogurt cakes without an oven, my family doesn't have to go out for breakfast anymore! - Photo 1.
- Add yogurt and mix until smooth, no lumps.
- Squeeze a few drops of orange or lemon juice in to remove the fishy smell of the eggs, then stir well. Add some raisins on top, then cover the bowl of dough with cling film, poke a few holes in the wrapper with a sharp toothpick. Put the bowl of dough into the steamer, steam for about 25 minutes, until the cake is cooked.

- Finished products:
- Yogurt cake has a sweet and sour taste, soft and delicious, especially delicious. This cake is very suitable for breakfast, this is also one of the dishes that support effective weight loss. Add it to your daily menu now!

Meringue cookie

INGREDIENTS:

- Chicken eggs 2
- Powdered sugar 110 gr
- Vanilla powder 1/2 teaspoon
- Food coloring 3 ml
- Lemon juice 1/2 teaspoon
- Hot water 500 ml

INSTRUCTIONS:

- Step 1: Boil whites
- First, you take a separate egg white in a bowl, be careful not to stick the yolk because the yolk contains a lot of fat, limiting the formation and easy air bubbles from the white. Thus, you will not be able to make delicious and successful cakes.
- Then, you pour 500ml of hot water into another bowl or bowl, then put the bowl of egg whites on top, put 110g of sugar in this bowl and stir until the sugar dissolves.
- Next, you add 1/2 teaspoon of vanilla powder with 1/2 teaspoon of lemon juice and continue to stir for another 3 minutes, then use a cooking thermometer to check, if the mixture reaches a temperature of 55 degrees Celsius is satisfactory.

- Step 2: Whip the whites
- You use an egg beater and beat the mixture on medium speed until the egg whites bubble, then until you see big bubbles, turn on the speed of the beat to the highest level.
- When the egg whites are in a stiff state, lift the whisk from the mixture if you see a vertical peak, it's done.

- Step 3: Shaping
- You divide the above mixture into different small bowls, then mix each cup with each food color you like.

- Next, you put the mixture in a bad catch bag, you pay attention to divide the mixture by color areas so that the finished product has the most beautiful color.
- Next, you use the ice cream bag prepared above and shape the cake to your liking.

- Step 4: Baking and drying cakes
- You preheat the oven at 170 - 190 degrees Celsius for 15 minutes before putting it in the oven, then put the cake in the oven at 90-100 degrees Celsius for 90 minutes. When baking for the specified time, turn off the oven, just turn on the light and leave the cake like that for another 5-10 minutes to dry the cake.

- Step 5: Finished product
- Banh Dat is a cake that is easy to remove from the parchment paper, crunchy and not moist inside. The cake has just been baked, smells like eggs, sweet and spongy, you can use it as a snack or decorate the cake.

Yogurt chiffon cupcake

INGREDIENTS:

- Egg yolks 4 piece (large eggs)
- Cooking oil 30 ml (do not use olive oil)
- Egg whites 4 pieces (large eggs)
- Yogurt 100 gr
- All-purpose flour 80 gr
- Cornmeal 15 gr
- Lemon juice 1.5 tsp
- Sugar 80 gr, salt 3 gr

INSTRUCTIONS:

- Step 1: Beat egg yolks:
- Mix egg yolks, 25g sugar and cooking oil in a bowl with a spatula.
- Add 1 teaspoon of lemon juice, yogurt to a bowl, mix well.
- Mix the flour and cornstarch and sift the flour into the egg bowl.

- Step 2: Beat egg whites:
- In another bowl, beat the egg whites with a whisk until frothy, then add a pinch of salt and 1/2 teaspoon of lemon juice.
- Beat on slow speed for about 30 seconds, then slowly add 55g of sugar and beat until stiff peaks form. If you don't have a whisk, you can beat it by hand.
- The whites when beaten will be very fluffy and "hard", feeling heavy in the hand. From the outside, the whites are smooth and shiny, and the whites feel soft. Lift the stick and see the egg stick to the top of the stick, absolutely no vibration or movement. Do not beat any longer because the whites are easily separated from the water, as discrete as soap bubbles.

- Step 3: Mix the mixture:
- Scoop 1/3 of the egg whites into the bowl of flour and yolk, mix well with a hand spatula to dilute the egg-flour mixture.
- Put the remaining 2/3 of the egg whites in a bowl and mix them gently, firmly and in one direction - do not reverse and be careful not to stir!

- Step 4: Baking:
- Divide the dough into a hard paper cup or cupcake mold lined with a soft paper cup, place in the oven 150 - 160 degrees Celsius (the oven has been preheated for 10-15 minutes) for 30-35 minutes or until the cake is golden, press Lightly on the surface of the cake, it immediately swells again, insert the test strip in the middle of the cake and pull it up to see that the stick is clean and dry.

- Step 5: Finished Products
- After removing the cake from the oven, you can eat it right away or wait for it to cool completely and then decorate it with fresh cream.
- The cake is soft, smooth, slightly sour, feels like it melts in your mouth!

Blueberry yogurt muffin

INGREDIENTS:

- 1 chicken egg
- Wheat flour 150 gr
- Fresh milk without sugar 120 ml
- Lemon juice 30 ml
- Olive oil 120 ml
- Sugar 120 gr
- Yogurt 100 gr
- Baking powder 5gr (baking powder)
- Salt 1/4 teaspoon
- Blueberries 130 gr

INSTRUCTIONS:

- Step 1: Mix the flour
- First, break the eggs into a large bowl and then add 120ml of olive oil, 80ml of unsweetened fresh milk, then add 120g of sugar and beat until the mixture is fluffy and blended.
- Next, add the yogurt and beat until the mixture is smooth. Sift in the flour, baking powder, and 1/4 teaspoon salt.
- Beat until a smooth, smooth dough is formed.

- Step 2: Blueberry filling
- Blueberries are washed, drained, then put in a bowl of flour, mix well. Line a muffin pan with a paper base, scoop the dough into each mold just enough to allow the cake to rise. Add some blueberries on top and sprinkle with brown sugar.

- Step 3: Bake
- Preheat the oven for 10 minutes at 180 degrees, put the cake in and bake for about 25 minutes, then check if the cake is dry, you can take it out and enjoy.

CONTENTS

Printed in Great Britain
by Amazon

24242245R00077